YOU ARE

ON

YOUR OWN

Inspirations To Self-Drive
Your Life To Success

Patrick Fynn Bondzi

As doctors, we have an arsenal of weapons after any. Antibiotics to kill infections, narcotics to fight pain, scalpels and retractors to remove tumours and cancers – to eradicate just the physical threats. For every other kind, you are on your own

Meredith Grey

ISBN: 978 – 9988 – 2 – 3194 – 1

Published by	STand-Out Innovations
	Accra, Ghana
Cover Design:	Osupong Design
Photography:	Filifili Studios
Typesetting, Printing and Binding:	Royal MediaTec Investment Ltd.
Editing:	Scribe Communications

For information or enquiries, feedback, booking or to place an order, please contact:

Phone: (+233) 0548628978, 0206718697

Email: patrickbondzi@gmail.com

Website: www.patrickfynn.com

LIKE this book on Facebook: You Are On Your Own

CONTENT

CHAPTER

ACKNOWLEDGMENT

I am highly indebted to some contributors for their sacrifices and support in my bid to make the publication of this book a reality.

I appreciate the editorial role played by a very supportive, prominent woman who insists on remaining anonymous. I cannot express how much grateful I am for her work on this piece. Scribe Communication also did a yeoman's job in the editing stage of this work; with particular mention of Kobina Ansah, who is the Chief Scribe. I deem it appropriate to honour Sena Quashie of Pulse Ghana and Miss Gladys Asantewaa Ohene for the proofreading.

My appreciation will be incomplete without making mention of Prof. Lade Worsunu who guided me to present a concept that is 'true'. May God bless you for giving me the privilege of being your mentee.

With gratitude, I would like to acknowledge the enormous support from friends and mates who have always encouraged me. I am also grateful to you, dear reader for patronising this book.

Above all, to God be the glory for endowing me with the talent and ability to make this see the light of the day. The Heavenly Father is the source of my being and daily downloads of inspiration.

DEDICATION

To my lovely Dad, Mum, Brother and Sister who have incessantly sustained and inspired my dreams. You make a wonderful family and I will continually make you proud!

FOREWORD

I have a friend who is always challenging me with this statement that, "If you want something done well, it is better done by yourself, rather than delegating it to someone". He simply calls it self-help. Over the years, this 'warning' has been vindicated in some experiences I have had.

It is not to say you do not have to seek help from somewhere, when you really need it. But do you live your entire life always depending on the help and support from others, without which you cannot be accomplished? Or will you spend your life looking out for people who should help you achieve that dream? So then, what happens to self-determination, self-trust, self-confidence and self-reliance?

This is exactly the influence YOU ARE ON YOUR OWN will have on you. It is a book that seeks to challenge you to be your own light. This is one book that makes you really appreciate the saying of Walter Walt Whitman, the American poet that, "Not I, nor anyone else can travel that road for you. You must travel it by yourself. It is not far. It is within your reach. Perhaps you have been on it since you were born, and did not know"

Sylvanus Bedzrah
Award-winning Writer,
Ghana.

ENDORSEMENTS

'Willpower', which has been defined by the American Heritage Dictionary as the strength of will to carry out one's decisions, wishes or plans is a gift God has given to every one of us. We are all free to decide what we want to do with our lives.

Whatever you amount to, on this earth and before God will depend on how you will use this power. Learn this and more from a fine burgeoning writer, Patrick Fynn.

I recommend this material as a life-changer that will guide your steps to success.

Richard Densu,
Head of Enterprise Business, MTN South Sudan
Founder and Chairman, Eagles and Eaglets

YOU ARE ON YOUR OWN is one informative masterpiece every young person should read, at least, once in their lifetime. Our lives are supposed to be in our hands, not in the hands of others. We are on our own!

Kobina Ansah,
Writer

YOU ARE ON YOUR OWN is a must read for anyone who is desirous of realising his/her destiny in life. This interesting and insightful book shares scintillating snippets on how one can create the best life now; enforcing the need to live life by choice and not by mere chance. In fact, the title says it all.

Your choice is your voice in life and once you make one, you are on your own. So make your life count with the right choices.

Gamel Sankarl
Author, Inspirational Speaker, Biomedical Scientist

PREFACE

The world we are living in is extremely competitive and challenging. In the midst of the pressures, people start to doubt themselves. It is therefore not uncommon to find individuals giving up on their abilities when they encounter failure.

Maybe this is because a lot of people do not seem to be aware of the fact that our success in the various spheres of life are tied to our efforts and ability to make the most out of ourselves.

Unlike soccer, our lives are pretty much like a race; a race in which the whole team is founded on the shoulders of one man. There's nobody there to bail you out of your mishap, even if you meant to save the world.

It is in this light that this book is put together to inspire readers and empower them to be responsible for their lives. The words put together in this book will plant a feeling of trust in your own efforts and abilities.

YOU ARE ON YOUR OWN is a journey filled with awe and discovery. What makes you want to go on an experience is to discover more of life. This journey will therefore align you with patterns of stimuli to react to what the world brings forth, so you can design, create and shape your own lives.

How do you break through to the life that you really desire and deserve? Have you found yourself drifting, and beginning to believe that the world controls your life and destiny? How about doing the all the things you have always dreamt of and wanted to do? These are the questions you should be asking yourself.

The concept does not discredit our reliance to God as religious beings, neither does it claim our independence of His sustenance. The import of this book isn't to say that we live on an island or are independent of the control and enablement of the Supreme Being. Rather, the exposure made in this book draws a line between Man and Man, attempting to make the individual less self-reliant on other people.

The old saying that 'God helps him who helps himself' is true in the sense that the Higher Aid refuses to come to the assistance of one who is not willing to strike out of him to do his best. Hence, instead of complaining about your circumstances, you will appreciate the need to rather get busy and create some new ones, even in despair.

The world is always trying to steal our attention and energy from the things that make our lives matter. The questions are simple: are you where you really want to be, or are you at a stage where you are not willing to buy into the theory that you have no choice? Are you at a point where you do not want the environment to become the factor that defines who you are? Are you at a place where it is time to lead and not just follow? Are you where God wants you to be? If the answer to all these questions is, "yes", then this book is the material you need to translate all these desires into reality.

It is my prayer and earnest hope that having been affected by the stimulation in this book, you will step into your power and nurture a bigger dream. Follow it up with calculated risks and deliberate action steps. Have no doubt about yourself.

Let's make a journey to unleash the beast in us!

Patrick Fynn Bondzi
Accra, Ghana

INTRODUCTION

I was always looking outside myself for strength and confidence but it comes from within. It was here all the time
– Anna Fred

There is a lie, prowling like a virus within the mind of humanity. That lie is that there's just not enough good to go around, and that we may need to rely on others who may be born with a silver spoon in their mouths. It has enslaved people to live in fear and the reckless desire to continually depend on others for sustenance.

But the truth is that, there's more than enough good for mankind – and each and every one of us should yearn for the best. There are more than enough creative ideas. There's more than enough power. There are more than enough dreams unrealized. All of these begin to come through a mind that is aware of its aptitude.

The splendour of this simple logic is that, being on your own cannot in any way be associated with selfishness or greed.

Interestingly, when everyone starts to live from their hearts and go for what they want, they do not go for the same things. We don't, for instance, all want the same kind of husbands. We don't all want the same kind of qualifications. We don't all want the same kind of houses, cars, food etc. No same experiences! You are the only one who wants the things you want.

Successful people are not gifted with success. The world doesn't enrich people by default. They work hard and succeed on plan.

Hence, it's imperative for you to live your life with action; with passion. Don't wait for it to happen. Make it happen! Make your own future. Make your own hope. Make your own love. And whatever your beliefs may be, honour your creator. Don't sit in idleness waiting for grace to come down from upon high. Do what you can to make grace happen right now; right down here on earth.

There's an arsenal of weapons for every threat in the world – antibiotics to kill the infection, narcotics to relieve the pain, scalpels and retractors to remove tumours and cancers. There are those remedies to salvage these physical threats. But for your problems, they are for you to face them – alone!

Face them! Show no emotion. Feel no pain. It's hard to resist the natural current; the downward pull but you need to. No one else can do it for you.

You are on your own and you know what you do. And you will decide where you go – Dr. Seuss.

A lot of people under certain conditions have had their lives collapsed around them. They work themselves into exhaustion only to see failure. Relationships are in turmoil. Others are going through a great deal of disappointment from trusting and having confidence in people. If only they knew they are in charge of their happiness, their lives would turn around.

You may have thought your way into negativity and misery. You have thought your way into holding on to someone that you broke up with and you are still sad, miserable and can't move on with your life. Your problem is, even when positive people are trying to give you good energy, you have tricked your mind to turn every positive thing into something negative.

I want to lay some reality on you.

It's all in the mind. Change your mind and it will change your life. You just have to wake up. You just have to break that spell of negative thinking. Break through. Take your life into your hands.

God is not done with you. That is why you are still here. Your life is like a nursery bed in a garden. Just beneath the surface is a sprouting seed about ready to break through. It's about time you blocked the shadows of the past from darkening the doorstep of your future. Stop looking for reasons to be unhappy. Focus on the things you do have, and the reasons you should be happy, for you are loved. You are wonderfully made. You are beautiful. You have a purpose, you are a masterpiece. God has a plan for you. You are living. You occupy space. You are matter, so you matter!

CHAPTER 1

YOUR DESTINY ACCORDING TO GOD'S PURPOSE

'Before I formed you in the womb I knew you. Before you were born, I set you apart...' – Jeremiah 1:4-5, The Bible (KJV).

Fate and Destiny - God's Sovereignty and an Individual Plan

Lest we get any wrong idea, God is sovereign. Only He is the supreme master of our fate. God is, therefore, in control of everything. He remains in control even when it seems like everything is out of control.

Our lives are no accident. The all-wise, all-powerful God has a plan for our lives. Undoubtedly, all holy books speak of a divine plan that is wise and benevolent. God's providence is in His will to bring about His original plan for creation.

Keep in mind that your destiny is a customized life God has ordained and thus, equipped you to accomplish great things. This, He does so as to bring to Himself the greatest glory. Ultimately, He wants to achieve the maximum expansion of His kingdom.

Everything that happens in the world is made to work out according to God's purpose. Evil exists, but it can't thwart God's providence.

'The king's heart is in the hand of the LORD; He directs it like a watercourse wherever He pleases' – Proverbs 21:1, The Bible.

God's sovereignty reaches even to a plan for our individual lives. This is illustrated in the calling of Jeremiah—before the prophet was even born. David also recognized that the Lord had a plan for him.

"Your eyes saw my unformed body. All the days ordained for me were written in your book before one of them came to be" (Psalm 139:16).

We can have a tall list of several other examples of characters whose lives were carefully moulded by God. He always has a purpose for mankind. It can therefore, be said conclusively that, as humans, we are brought forth with a purpose.

Many people live their lives based on scripts written by teachers, scripts written by the trends of society, scripts written by the government and its economy. They always fail to discover their true, unique purpose in life.

The question is, "What is your purpose?" Without purpose you can never become a self-motivated individual. You cannot be on your own!

Before you proceed to discover how to drive your life to a fulfilling end, ask yourself, "What does God want you to do with your life? Are you doing it?" If you are not yet sure about what destiny God has for you, it doesn't have to remain a mystery any longer. By seeking a closer relationship with your Creator, you can discover and fulfil what He has created you to do!

Ask God to reveal to you your passion. You have been created with specific desires and motivations. Paying attention to those will help you discover what you are passionate about. Ask yourself questions such as, "What captures my attention the most? What makes me feel alive? What would I choose to do if I could do any kind of work?" Once you have identified what you are passionate about, consider how your passion connects to eternal values.

Your Destiny Is In Your Hand

We are spiritually created beings made to rely on God. That is His nature for us. He is there to be an answer to the conflicts in our lives. We are made to carry out nothing without Him.

God's help towards materializing our purpose makes a turn-around to become our own ability to rise up and build! In Exodus 14:15, as Israel was standing at the foot of the Red Sea with the enemy right on their tail, Moses cried out to God. God then says to Moses, "Why are you standing there looking to me? I have told you, everything you need is in your hand. Go forward; stop standing around – get busy. Raise your arm. Take what is in your hand and stretch it out in front of you."

Just as Moses did, we have to look up to God and coordinate our spiritual vision with what has been placed in our hand. When God tells us to move on and to use what we have in our hand, we need to be aware that we have a lot more than a big stick. Our destinies are in our hands!

So… take what you have and stretch it out in the direction you need to move in your life.

It is God's promise to part the Red Sea in your life. However, it is your duty to walk through it – on your own. You will not be walking in someone else's footprints; you will be making your own. You may be leaving footprints where they may have never been seen before. Go ahead and move forward. Everything you need is in your own hand. God has supplied you with all you need. Stretch out. Your destiny is in your hand!

Fate and Destiny - Our Free Will

He has chosen to give us a free will. The Lord could have made all people like clones or robots to do His every bidding without a second thought. But the Bible teaches that man was created with the ability to make moral choices and that he is responsible for those choices. The fall of man was not a predetermined event in which Adam and Eve were helpless victims of a puppeteer-Master God.

On the contrary, they had the opportunity to choose obedience (with its attendant blessing) or disobedience (with its consequent curse). They knew what the result of their decision would be, and they were held accountable. How they exercised their free will changed the world. They were on their own!

This theme of being held accountable for our choices continues throughout scriptures. *"He who sows wickedness reaps trouble"* (Proverbs 22:8a). We sin because we choose to. We cannot blame fate, kismet, predestination or even God.

The Bible says in Ephesians 2:10,
'For we are God's masterpiece. He has created us anew in Christ Jesus, so we can do the good things he planned for us long ago'.

As discussed above, God gave you a unique mixture of spiritual gifts, passions, abilities, personality, and experiences. There's no one like you in the entire universe because, in reality, there's no one with your unique mix of talents. That's why your destiny is so unique. It's your destiny; not your mother's, not your father's, not your pastor's. It's your destiny!

But here's the painful part... you can miss God's destiny for your life. People do it all the time. In fact, you can go through your entire life and miss its real purpose — by your own choices. If you choose to chase the trivial things of life, you will miss it. And that is tragic.

Consider why it is important to start living according to your call. Living out your destiny will give you greater fulfilment, direction, stability, significance, identity, and provision in your life. Don't settle for less than the best life has for you— finding and fulfilling your destiny every day that you live.

9

God's will is not automatic. He allows us to make choices. Many of the things that happen to you are not the perfect will of the Supreme Being. If I got drunk, fell in a pool and drowned, that would not be God's will for my life. It would be my own doing. God has a destiny for your life but He will not force it on you. We have been given the free will to make choices. Hence, the onus lies on us to choose rightly.

You can have God's will for your life. Even when you mess up, God can turn disaster into destiny. It is never too late to have his perfect will in your life. Just pray, "God, I want your purpose for my life," and you will not miss it — no matter where you have been. He will get you in line with His purpose. He wants you to fulfil your destiny more than you do!

In summary, the Bible teaches that God is in charge. At the same time, He has given us the freedom to choose.

Your life is not an accident. Before you were born, God wired you with certain ambitions, desires, and drives to play a particular role in history — one that only you can play.

CHAPTER 2

YOUR OWN THOUGHTS CREATE YOU

"As man thinketh in his heart, so he is". - Proverbs 23:7,
The Bible

Why is it that just a minute fraction of the world's population chalk massive successes in finance, politics, arts, religion et cetera, and make the greatest feats while majority of the people continue to wallow in drawbacks?

It's not an accident. They understand something. They apply certain key principles to their lives. They keep special 'codes' majority of people are blind to.

I tried tracing this philosophy back into history. I started a journey of digging deep into this mystery. I caught a glimpse of this great secret through interactions with successful people who are making an impact on society.

With this secret, you can have, do or become anything you want. It frees you from a long-standing mental slavery and gives you the conviction that you can exercise full control over your life.

The big secret is in **your thoughts**.

Whatever the mind can conceive and believe, the mind can –
Napoleon Hill

12

There is a natural law of attraction that brings you the things you muse on; whether or not they are positive. If you sit imagining a mountain of debt and feeling terrible about it, that is the signal you are putting into the physical realm of the universe. This law of attraction is really obedient and precise. It reciprocates your thoughts. Anytime your thoughts are flowing, it is operational. You literally call imaginations into existence as you make space for them in your thoughts.

You have to hold on to your thoughts. You have to make it absolutely clear what you want. You are what you think. So ordinarily, if you think it in your head, you hold it in your hand
 The hard truth is that no other person gets to do this exercise of imagination for you, no matter how much they would want to.

Creation is an on-going process. You draw everything to yourself – the people, the job, the health, the circumstances, the joy, the debt, the car that you may want to drive, etc. And you move them to yourself like a magnet. Your life is a physical manifestation of the thoughts that go on in your head.

What you think about, you bring about – Lisa Nicholas, Author

Here's the problem – most people are thinking about what they do not want, and they wonder why it shows up over and over again. The funny thing is that everything that's around them now, including the things they are complaining about, have been attracted by their thoughts! They are not the fault of a reckless driver, an infection or a relative. They are the situations they successfully created, merely by thinking.

People hate to hear this. They dislike having their accusing fingers turned back at them. They quickly retort to these with 'I can't be responsible for that car accident that messed me up. I didn't attract this failure,' etc.

The hard truth to accept, however, is that you are 100% responsible for what happens in your life and with your life. Most of us draw disappointments by default. We harbour the false assumption that we have no control over them.

All that we are is the result of what we have thought. It is founded on our thoughts and made up of our thoughts –
Buddha

Imagination Is Everything

The question I would like to ask you to consider is, "Are the results you have in your life what you really wanted? Are they worthy of you?" If they are not, this moment will be the right time to change them, because you have the power to.

Robert Collier, an American author once said, "All power is from within and is, therefore, under your own control". Humans have not yet explored and exploited this powerfully powerful power for the good of mankind. When the Good Books says, '*He that is in me is greater than he that is in the world*', the similitude to be drawn from that quote is, '*the power that is in you is greater than that which is in the world*'.

The popular legend of Disney's Aladdin story is a perfect analogy for this theme. It teaches us there's absolutely no limits to whatsoever you wish. Like Aladdin, you carry with you a very, very, very big genie.

Inside a cave, Aladdin rubs the lamp and inadvertently unleashes Genie, the supernatural creature who expresses unflinching willingness to grant his wishes. Aladdin is the one who always asks for what he wants. We have got the universe at large; which is this grand Genie. We can call it the 'Higher Self', which in this sense is your thoughts. It's interesting how the genie always says one thing, 'Your wish is my command'.

'Behind me is an infinite power. Before me is in an endless possibility. Around me is a boundless opportunity.' – Unknown Author

The obligation, therefore lies with you to decide what you want. Believe you can have it. Believe you deserve it. Believe it is possible for you. Close your eyes every day for several minutes and visualise having what you want. Feel it. Believe it is already yours. That is what I call unwavering faith!

Your job is to declare what you want from the catalogue of the universe's luxuries. Well, if cash is one of them, say how much you want to have. The universe does everything with zero effort. The grass doesn't strive to grow, you know.

'Imagination is everything. It is the preview of life's coming attractions' – Albert Einstein.

Just think and become. It is your life – your own life. In your mind, draw up good images of how you want it to be. When you want to change your circumstances you must first change your thoughts.

Henry Ford said, *'Whether you think you can or you can't, either way you are right.'*

You can never live and enjoy in the future you desire if you cannot see it for yourself today… in your mind's eye. It is no coincidence that the popular Ghanaian motivational speaker Emmanuel Dei-Tumi once said, *"We are in the era of Mind Power, not man power. Develop your mind!"*

Here is another thing. If you do not understand this principle, it does not mean you should reject it. You do not understand electricity probably, yet you enjoy the benefits of it. Do you know how it works? I have no idea how it works, but I do know this: you can light up your room with electricity.

There's a part of the brain that will say, "Hoh! This is a lie. This is impossible. It's unreal. These are mere philosophies". In applying this secret, you have to note that this 'tennis match' will go on for a while. It's a bitter pill to swallow, but once you accept the responsibility of governance for every happening of your life, it becomes the first significant step to an overwhelming life transformation.

A Mind of Mystery

The mind holds the central position in the life of every individual. It is the tool that coordinates the activities of all other elements of the human being. Every man's worth is determined and imprinted on the mind. Human beings lose their value and usefulness when their minds become faulty. We all know.

Your brain, which is the body's master console, is constantly working; and neither shuts down nor takes a vacation; from your nervous system and blood balances to your sexual functions that you have no conscious idea about. Your brain is the captain at the helm; creating, driving, balancing and maintaining you all the time.

Scientists know that when you have a thought, your brain makes chemicals that open what they refer to as windows. And when the thought is over, the window closes. There are chemicals that change your mood in any situation, under the control of the brain. Scientists call them Neuropeptides. When you have any thought, they alter you.

Now here's where it gets weird...

It has been discovered that your immune system has got specific loading docks for neuropeptides. In simple terms, your immune system is definitely listening to your emotional dialogue. Literally speaking, the private conversations you have with yourself have an upshot on your ability to fight germs. In summary, your immune cells' response is determined by your thoughts! Weird, but true.

17

Imagine the kind of attacks your immune system has to survive every day. If you think flesh-eating bacteria and killer viral influenzas are bad, well scientific research clearly proves that your worst immune attack is not microbes, but what you are thinking.

In medical science and the healing arts, the power of thoughts is clearly evident in the effects of placebo therapy. A placebo is a 'dummy medicine' that contains no active ingredient. In clinical practice, when we realise a patient's medical condition is not caused by a physical disorder, or has no recognisable source, placebos are administered to them.

For instance, ordinary water could be injected into hysteric patients. The therapy creates the perception of cure in them and excites their thoughts into believing they will get well. And almost all the time, it works! You get cured sometimes because you merely trusted and believed in the efficacy of the treatment. Cure is in your thoughts!

Disease thrives in a body that is in constant emotional distress. If you have a disease and you are focusing on it and you are talking to people about it, you are going to create more diseased cells. See yourself living in a perfectly healthy body. It is your own being, and you are on your own. So reform it your way.

Our thoughts create our bodies. How does it happen? What we believe and feel are continuously reassembling, reorganising and recreating our bodies. Our psychology is succinctly influencing our physiology to create disease; a feedback that we have an imbalanced perspective.

18

You are on your own, and so it your body's anatomical system –it heals itself. You can change your life, you can create yourself.

A clinical psychologist once said, 'Incurable means curable from within', meaning the dream that appears unachievable has got the achievements embedded inside of you. You can change your life and health yourself. You are on your own!

You may be bedridden for weeks, months or even years, with your condition accentuating futility. Doctors may refer to your disease state as incurable and terminal. That is the picture they see of you. That is what their intelligence will come up with – that you are a vegetable. But the main thing is what YOU think of your condition. The decider of your prognosis is your set of thoughts. With an intact mind, you can put things together again.

Here is what to do every morning. Wake up and evoke into your being how younger you want to be, even in your old age. Hold images of an energetic youthful self and there you have it! It's inexplicable, but it works.

If you have been there in mind, you can be there in the body. Just visualise where you want to be. There are physical consequences for everything you do, and now it appears true for even everything you think, too.

*Finally brethren, whatsoever things are true, whatever things are noble, whatever things are just, whatever things are lovely, whatever things are of good report, if there is any virtue and if there is anything praiseworthy, **think** on these things* – Philippians 4:8

CHAPTER 3

FACING YOUR FEARS

The greatest thing to fear is your own fears – Franklin Roosevelt

In the animated movie, '*The Croods*', there lived a family that spent most of its lifetime in a cave, in the dark; night after night; day after day. Their lives were tied to the strings of perpetual fear, always saying to themselves, "Never not be afraid" and sat in the deception that "fear keeps us alive".

This cave-dwelling clan was led by a patriarch, Grug, who confined his family and constantly monitored them to avoid anything unfamiliar. They took a cue from the extinction of their neighbouring families who were all killed by one calamity or the other. All that the Croods knew was fear.

One of the Croods, Eep, wanted to break free of this monotonous boundary of 'safety'. For her, restraint was soul-stifling and a waste of the already short life span they were bequeathed. While being capricious, Eep encountered Guy, an autonomous individual who had learned to utilise his surrounding to survive, as opposed to avoiding them. Guy was able to trek long distances by making shoes from what appeared to be feet of an elephant. He was also able to create fire, unlike the Croods who dreaded unfamiliar things as such.

The destruction of the Crood's cave came following an earthquake. The family was thrust into a relationship with Guy, the one willing to take risks. Through the scuffles, they had to succumb to his daring ideas to help the family make another settlement in a land far away.

Emmanuel Dei Tumi once said, *"Never be afraid of taking unfamiliar paths because sometimes they are the ones that take us to the best places"*.

You are like teabag. You never know what you are made of until you are in hot water. You are stronger and better than you can imagine. There are times when we need to face the situation and take the appropriate action. If you allow people to exploit you physically, mentally, emotionally or financially, they will continue to do so, until you are crushed under their manipulations.

Many people do not know that we gain strength, courage and confidence by every experience as we stop to look fear in the face. To be able to say to yourself, "I have lived through this horror; I can take the next thing that comes along", you must do the things you cannot do.

Fear Is Not To Be Fled

To escape fear, you have to go through it, not around it –
Richie Norton

Like Jaguar Paw!

The popular 2006 American epic adventure, *Apocalypto*, illustrates fear as its theme in the story of Jaguar Paw of the Mayan tribe.

In the beginning, Jaguar Paw together with his father, Flint Sky and some other men encountered a group of demoralised refugees seeking to make a pass though their land to seek asylum elsewhere. Flint Sky says to his son, "Those people in the forest, what did you see on them? Fear. Deep fear! They were infected by it. Did you see? Fear is a sickness. It will crawl into the soul of anyone who engages it. It has tainted your peace already. I did not raise you to see you live with fear. Strike it from your heart. Do not bring it into our village".

This is important. The father's attempt to inoculate the effect of giving up to fear makes a remarkable effect in Jaguar's life as seen in how he went through the ordeal of securing a life for himself and his family against all odds.

Jaguar Paw wakes up the next morning to see his tribe being attacked. His people do not stand a chance of survival. Presumably, this is the same group that shattered the lives of the harried people they met the previous day. Jaguar takes his own life into his hands and defends it with the last drop of his blood.

I really appreciate the magnitude of courage applied in the entire struggle, motivated by his burning desire to save his family – as the tribe was near extinction. The purity and simplicity of this character's struggle is worth emulating.

A life-threatening moment comes when Jaguar Paw survives the jump from the huge waterfall. Standing on the bank of the river, he springs up with a body full of adrenaline and yells to the men pursuing him: "I am Jaguar Paw, son of Flint Sky! My Father hunted this forest before me. My name is Jaguar Paw. I am a hunter. This is my forest and my sons will hunt it with their sons when I am gone. Come after me if you have the balls!"

For any man watching this scene, it certainly is the golden manly moment when you start nodding your head and pump your fist, screaming, 'Yes!' And yes indeed, this is when the hunter faces his fear and begins to pick off his enemies one by one, ultimately defeating each one of them. Each and every one of them!

Fear is one of the most destructive things you will ever encounter in your life. *Apocalypto* is an amazing piece from which we can draw inspiration to inhibit the power of fear in our bid to push the 'You are on your own' agenda.

'Never bend your head. Always hold it high. Look the world straight in the eye' – Hellen Keller

Most people only pay attention to the final products of successful entrepreneurs. They say things like "I can never be like them" or "They got lucky". Unfortunately, what they do not see is what the achievers have overcome – the daily struggles, the rejections, the disappointments, the betrayals, the rumours, the criticisms, the empty bank accounts, the lonely nights while trying to make their visions into reality.

The only difference between the one who quits and the one who doesn't is that one of them shows up every day. One grabs the bull by its horn no matter how long it appears while the other flees the challenge.

Fruitful people work every day. They strive every day. They learn every day. They improve every day. They toil every day. They never give up. They do all these even though they feel like quitting every day. Eventually they have become who they are today!

The day you do not give up on your dreams is the day you will reach your goals. Never take to your heels. Quitters never win and winners never quit. Encounters are deceptive at first sight. We all know the David-and-Goliath story, too. Muse on it.

Twenty years from now, you will be more disappointed by the things that you didn't do than the ones you did. You will not be able to forgive yourself for your failure to push though the hard times.

Being successful doesn't mean everything is perfect. It means that you have decided to look beyond the imperfections. Hope for the best and stick with it day in and day out. Even when you get tired, even when you want to walk away… don't! You are a pioneer. Nobody ever said it will be easy.

"Always do what you are afraid to do." – Ralph Waldo Emerson

Fear stands for **F**alse **E**vidence that **A**ppears **R**eal. It is the main thing that holds you back from believing in yourself again more than anything else. Do the things that frighten you. Take one small step, then another. Action builds courage. Tell yourself, "This fear will pass." Your world expands as your courage and willingness to grow expands. Open up your world today to face your fear.

Opportunity knocks, but we're too deaf to hear. Put to death our fears. bring to life our dreams - M.anifest

I draw admonition from these quotes which you will find useful, too. These words inspire me a lot:

1. *Each of us must confront our own fears... must come face to face with them. How we handle our fears will determine where we go with the rest of our lives. To experience adventure or to be limited by the fear of it. – Judy Blume*

2. *Inaction breeds doubt and fear. Action breeds confidence and courage. If you want to conquer fear, do not sit home and think about it. Go out and get busy. – Dale Carnegie*

3. *You gain strength, courage and confidence by every experience in which you really stop to look fear in the face. You are able to say to yourself, 'I have lived through this horror. I can take the next thing that comes along.' You must do the thing you think you cannot do. – Eleanor Roosevelt*

4. *He who is not every day conquering some fear has not learned the secret of life. – Ralph Waldo Emerson*

5. *We should all start to live before we get too old. Fear is stupid. So are regrets. – Marilyn Monroe*

6. *Fear keeps us focused on the past or worried about the future. If we can acknowledge our fear, we can realize that right now we are okay. Right now, today, we are still alive, and our bodies are working marvellously. Our eyes can still see the beautiful sky. Our ears can still hear the voices of our loved ones. – Thich Nhat Hanh*

7. *Avoiding danger is no safer in the long run than outright exposure. The fearful are caught as often as the bold. – Helen Keller*

8. *One of the greatest discoveries a man makes, one of his great surprises, is to find he can do what he was afraid he couldn't do. – Henry Ford*

9. *Don't fear failure so much that you refuse to try new things. The saddest summary of life contains three descriptions: could have, might have, and should have. ~ Unknown*

10. *Too often, we allow fear, worry, and doubt to dominate and define our lives. We allow them to steal our joy, our sleep, and our precious dreams – Tess Marshall*

CHAPTER 4

BE THYSELF

Be yourself. Everyone else is taken – Oscar Wilde

According to Advanced Life Skills, the phrase, 'find myself' gets over 5 million searches per month in Google. That shows how common it is for people to feel disconnected from their true selves and how interested they are in re-establishing that long lost connection. How about you? Are you willing to be your true self in a more complete, meaningful way?

Even for those who feel somewhat in touch with their true nature, the constant barrage of carefully crafted advertisements coupled with the pressure of external expectations can make it extremely difficult to maintain that core association. Figuring how to be your self is a necessary step to take. However, to continue to be yourself day in and out, you need to stay grounded and connected.

We experiment with a variety of identities from childhood. During these formative years, we have no idea who we actually are or who we will become, so we take our cues from those around us. Because we are impressionable, it is only natural that we try on new versions of ourselves at fairly regular intervals. The less inhibited we are, the more readily we will try to initiate whatever appeals to us at the moment.

Be the type of person you want to meet – Dutchess Roz

Conversely, the expectation of those around us also exert a strong influence on our identity. Many of the choices we think we have made in life were probably programmed into us by the expectations of those whose approval we craved.

It is a very well-known fact that for anyone to succeed in life, they must believe in themselves. We need to have confidence in our abilities because our inner faith will create our external results. People easily lose faith in themselves when they encounter setbacks, failure and fear.

When you lack confidence in yourself, everyone else will, too. **Not many people live the life that they have always wished to have lived. They give up on their life goals as soon as they encounter the first setback. One of the main causes of this is that they do not believe in themselves!**

There is this story of some goats returning from the bush to their home. A little boy playing in the bush decided to have fun with them so he tied a rope to a tree across the path. He went the other side of the path and held the rope a foot high.

When the animals got to the line, the first one jumped across it. Another goat followed. After the fifth goat had jumped, the little boy lowered the rope to the ground. However, all the other goats continued to jump when they got to that particular spot. Why? They saw others jump so they equally did same for no reason!

This story is as true to the goats as it is to you and me. There are many times we tend to jump because everybody is jumping. We want to go into a career because everybody is going there, too. We want to start a business because somebody has started it, too. We want to go to a certain school or pursue a particular course because everybody is doing it, too. At work, we want to work the way everybody is working. The list is endless.

You do not have to jump because others are doing so. You need to have a compelling reason to do so. Set your own standards at the work place. You do not have to conform to the ways of others. Set your own life goals. Do not be 'remote-controlled' by others. Do not always copy what others are always doing. Sit down and figure out who you are and act from that uniqueness. The world does not reward copy cats!

What they call, 'order of the day' should not order your life. Your life's resolutions should not be according to how others are jumping. Be original. When it comes to integrity, we live in a society where 'what is said' and 'what is done' are always opposite. Don't conform.

Conformity is the first child of mediocrity. When you conform, you lose your uniqueness, your self-worth and the creativity in you. If the world will change, it starts from me being me and you being you. It starts from us living our lives in our uniqueness.

When Ghana's award-winning rapper, Sarkodie started his career with his unique trademark, he was slapped with tonnes of criticisms that doing music solely in his local parlance will render him unsung forever. Even at the climax of his career when he appeared on international scenes, he continued to portray an inimitable personality of true ingenuity. His quest to keep an original brand devoid of adulteration has made him what he is today.

To be yourself in a world that is constantly trying to make you something else is the greatest accomplishment – Ralph Waldo Emerson

Being yourself is very difficult if you believe that you are worthless or underserving which, of course, isn't true. Make it a habit to cultivate positive feelings about yourself as a person. Train your mind to see the good in yourself. Bruce Burton suggests,

'Nothing splendid has ever been achieved except by those who dared believe that something inside of them was superior to circumstances.'

Why compare yourself to others? No one in the entire world can do a better job of being you than you.

There are several fables of that have sold the idea that every individual should be allowed to pursue his or her own strengths. Let's share one of those allegories.

All animals decided to establish a school and they selected a board consisting of Mr. Elephant, Mr. Kangaroo and Mr. Monkey. These fellows held a meeting to agree upon the modus operandi of the institution.

"What shall the animals' children be taught in this school? That is the question," asked Mr. Monkey. "They should be taught to climb trees. All my relatives will serve as teachers."

31

"No, indeed!" shouted the other two in chorus. "That would never be taught as such."

"They should be taught to jump," cried the Mr. Kangaroo with emphasis. "All of my relatives will be glad to teach them."

The elephant vehemently opposed and suggested. "Teach them to look wise."

The debate spanned for hours. None of them would yield in to the other's suggestion. When it was obvious there was no chance to agree, they all became angry and decided not to have the animal school at all.

There exists so much folly in trying to run all kinds of individuals through the same mould, with the vain hope of bringing all to the same standard of uniformity. Nothing gets achieved. We need to be the persons we are meant to be. A weakness in some area should not induce feelings of debilitating inferiority.

Everybody is a genius but if you judge a fish by its ability to climb a tree, it will leave its whole life believing it is stupid
– Albert Einstein

Take Your Gaze Off Others

Someone wrote…

"Last week, I drove into a fuel station for a refill. My car has a fuel tank capacity of about 60 litres. While the pump attendant filled my tank, a motorcyclist also rode in to the second pump. Before I knew it, the motorcycle was full and the rider rode off while I was still at the pump.

I got in before the motorcyclist but he left before me. It suddenly occurred to me that it would be absolutely silly of me to think "I got here before him. How come he is leaving before me?" Why? Our capacities are not the same."

The truth is there are times in life when we get stuck in our tracks. Those who came in behind us have gone ahead of us; those who learnt from you seem to have outran you; those who graduated years after you are now the ones calling the shot and it seems as though you are stuck.

Could it just be that your capacity is bigger than theirs? Could it be that your own assignment needs longer preparation? Could it be that your character is being formed for the task ahead?

People will often say, "my mates are doing this, my mates have done that, my mates have this, my mates are now…but I'm still here doing, having nothing". However, it is important to know that you spent nine months of formation in your mother's womb alone and you were given birth to alone even if you are a twin. Therefore never classify anyone as your *mate*.

View yourself as God sees you. God has created you to be a masterpiece, and that's how He sees you. As a masterpiece, you are rare, special, valuable, named, and known. God's dealings with your life is never an estimation of what is happening in the life of your friend or colleagues. Yours is very personal and unique and should never be an estimation of physical and tangible things.

Take your gaze off other people's path and concentrate on the race. You will earn your own medal.

Never envy anyone. Do not ever wish you were someone. What people have is what they have toiled for. Some have put their lives on the line to be where they are, and to merely wish to be that which they have struggled for, is lethal.

A lot happens behind closed doors before people show you the beautiful parts of their lives. Some have very nasty backstages you have no idea of. Behind their smiles are unwholesome stories they wouldn't share with you. You either accept what you are or also go through the painful process of reformation. Simply be yourself!

If rose smells better than cabbage, it doesn't mean it can make a better stew. Why compare yourself to others? I repeat that no one in the entire world can do a better job of being you than you.

You should rather develop and make use of your gifts and talents. You also have your own strength. Search for it and

34

build. Success is an outward evidence of what we truly are within.

The less you focus on others, the more time you get to focus on things that are important to you. So stop trying to please others. The truth is, you will never be able to please everybody, so why try? Prove yourself to yourself, not others.

Your worth is dependent on no one else's approval. When you are busily trying to please others, you are not honouring your true self. You are not honouring God, too.

Believe in yourself, and the rest will fall into place. Have faith in your own abilities, work hard and there is nothing you cannot accomplish." – Brad Henry

You are valuable and irreplaceable. If you are told otherwise, do not believe it. This is one of the most important things that can help you get that belief and confidence back. All the energy, power, courage, strength and confidence is within you.

Spend time with yourself to assess it, whether it be through meditation or activities that make you trust in yourself again. How can you expect anyone else to enjoy your company if you don't enjoy your own company? Give more to yourself by filling yourself to fullness then you can overflow in giving. Here's a question to muse on; do you treat yourself the way you treat others?

There's something so magnificent about YOURSELF. The 'Me' part of life hasn't yet been explored by many, thus we fail to love ourselves and admire the barns of goodness compressed in us. I'm not talking about conceit. I'm talking about respect for the SELF.

"Everything in the universe is within you. Ask all from yourself." – Rumi

Be Yourself
By Ellen Bailey
Why would you want to be something else?
When you could be better by being yourself
When you pretend to be something you are not
When you have something they haven't got
Cheating yourself of the life you have to live
Deprives others of that only which you can give
You have much more to offer by being just you
Than walking around in someone else's shoes
Trying to live the life of another is a mistake
It is a masquerade; noting more than fake
Be yourself and let your qualities show through
Others will love you more for being just you.
Remember that God loves you just as you are
To Him you are already a bright shining star
Family and friends will love you more too
If you spent time practising just being you.

CHAPTER 5
THE MASTER BREWER

"Some people want it to happen, some wish it would happen, others make it happen" – Michael Jordan

A story is told of an elderly carpenter who was ready to retire and told his boss of his plans to live a more leisurely life with his wife and children. He would miss the pay check, but he needed to retire. They could get by.

The contractor was sorry to see such a good, hardworking worker go. He asked him to build just one more house as a personal favour. The carpenter consented. With time, however, it was obvious that he was not willing to do that particular task. He resorted to shoddy workmanship and used inferior materials. It was an unfortunate way to end a dedicated career. When he had finished putting up the structure, his employer came to inspect the house. He handed the front-door key to him saying, "This is your house. It is my gift to you." He was shocked. What a shame! If only he had known he was building his own house, he would have done it all so differently.

So it is with us. We build our lives a day at a time, often putting less than our best into the building. In our utmost shock we realize we have to live in the house we have shoddily built. If we could do it over again, we would have done it much differently. But we cannot go back!

You are the carpenter of your life. Each day you hammer a nail, place a board, or erect a wall. Your attitudes and the choices you make today build your house tomorrow.

Build wisely. It's your life, and you are on your own. Pastor Chris Oyakhilome in one of his sermons mentioned,

> *"You cannot change yesterday but you can do something today to change tomorrow. None of you was born to be poor; you may have been born poor, you are not meant to be poor".*

A number of people have long lived with the deception that another person is somehow responsible for the events that happen to them. Their decisions, actions and inactions are somewhat left at the mercy of friends, parents, pastors, teachers, etc. It is not uncommon to find people tie their destinies to the strings of others.

Our decisions construct our destiny. Anthony Robbins, an American motivational speaker and author said, *'It is in the moments of our decisions that our destiny is shaped'.*

Here's where we make good use of the popular poem of Prof. Lade Worsonu, a prominent figure on the Ghanaian literary and academic landscape:

The Master Brewer
There is a distillery in our brains
Its cane and malt its hops and grains
Are the stuff our lives are made of
Blizzard or snow, bush fire or draught
Matches won by penalty shoot-out
Fortunes lost at toss of a coin
Over these, and their like, you are no doyen,
The fuel for the distillery?
Your emotions. Willy nilly

You stake the fire as you vent your spleen
And another drawn drips into the vat-unseen.
The master brewer is not the stars
Not yet the gods. He is you, your very self.
The final brew has no choice, it must be
Bitter bile or sweet honey. But you can choose
The magic potion which vouchsafes the taste;
Your intentions, your memories, your reflections.

Now let's digest this…
The poem is a philosophical piece likening the human body to some sort of industry, constantly at work, brewing. It is, thus, fed in by the stuff our lives are made of.

A doyen is a master of a group. Rightly, the things that are mentioned are outside his distillery: the blizzard, snow, fires, drought, and the match-winning penalty shootout or the loss fortune over the toss of a coin. In effect, man has more authority over himself than over things outside him.

In the last stanza, Lade tells us how the taste of the final brew depends solely on us, not the gods or stars. Whether it is bitter bile or sweet honey depends on the 'magic potion' we put in it. With that position, he concludes that it is the make of our intentions, memories and reactions. The more positive our mind-set, the sweeter the brew from your distillery; the more positive life becomes for you.

The statement, '*But you can choose*' emphasises that even though we may have little control over happenings such as the outcome of coin toss, we have authority over our reaction to the aftermaths plus how they affect us. But you can choose!

You are in charge of how you feel – Eleanor Rosevelt

You have often given people the honourable opportunity to create your happiness, and many times they have failed to create it the way you wanted them to. Fact is, only one person can be in charge of your joy and your bliss. And that's you – you are on your own!

The people closest to you even do not have the power to create your happiness. Your joy lies within you!

The Brewer Decides

The greatest setback in becoming the chauffeurs of our life is the hesitation in making life-changing decisions. Sometimes a split-second decision could be your turn-around. Although you are the master brewer, you are not in charge of your life until you are in charge of your decisions.

Decisions!

Okay, let's do this…
Put a frog in a vessel of water and start heating it. As the temperature of the water rises, the frog is able to adjust its body temperature accordingly. The frog keeps on adjusting with increase in temperature. Just when the water is about to reach boiling point, the frog is not able to adjust anymore. At that point the frog is unable to jump out.
The frog tries to jump but is unable to do so, because it has lost all its strength in adjusting with the rising water temperature. Very soon the frog dies.

41

What killed the frog? Many of us would say the boiling water. But the truth is, **what killed the frog was its own inability to decide when it had to jump out!**

We all need to adjust with people and situations, but we need to be sure when we need to adjust and when we need to confront or face our fears. We have to decide when to jump. Let us jump while we still have the strength.

You can't let other people tell you who you are. You have to decide that for yourself - Michael Jordan

What do you really want? Resolve in yourself what your dreams are. Sit down and write it on a piece of paper. Tell yourself how you want your life to be. You have a higher self which is at your service. Remember Aladdin and the Genie story?

The Brewer's Ingredients

When the philosopher says you are the master brewer, it literally means you are responsible for what goes into you and what comes out of you. It's like a two-way catheter.

Sounds too bizarre? Pick an orange as you read on. Make a puncture on it and squeeze. What comes out? Orange juice! Why does it come out? Because that's what is inside. The orange is you.

People poke you. Friends disappoint you. Folks infuriate you. They may say things you do not like…and what comes out of you is anger, hatred, revenge, depression. Then immediately you say, "They made me feel that way! They hurt my feelings".

Just like the orange, these feelings come out of us because they were already inside. If you want to change your life, you need to look inside, so that when life squeezes you, the only thing that comes out of you is understanding and love.

As you have the privilege of cooking your inner being, infuse yourself with positivity only.

There's always a distinction between the exceptional graduate and the average one. It is not the schools they attended but the choices they make. Whatever your level is presently, you can reposition for a better tomorrow.

Whatsoever we throw into the ocean of life is what it will vomit for us on the shores of life – Ikechukwu Izuakor

In our human body, the amazing piece of engineering marvel, the most complicated organ is our brain; a machine that never becomes tired. It sometimes, however, gets sluggish per the food it gets. Computer experts use the acronym 'GIGO' to illustrate the fact that the computer can process only the information it is given. GIGO (garbage in, garbage out) is a concept common to computer scientists and mathematicians. It means the quality of output is determined by the quality of input.

The axiom holds true for our minds also. If you feed it with healthy, nourishing food, it will grow strong and active but if you restrict it to a regular diet of junk nutrition, you will become unhealthy, negative and unproductive.

A lot of scrap materials are deposited into our lives through various mediums: TV, radio, the internet, associations with people and what have you. All these and more influence us in various ways.

Your mind is a storehouse of facts, figures, images, beliefs and opinions. The supply in your storehouse has been stuffed since childhood and added on by acquaintances. It is further supplied by what you read, what you watch and what you experience. That creates the assumptions that drive the decisions you make. Input controls choice. Choice drives actions. Actions determine results.

A lot of failures in our decisions are due to faulty, incomplete, imprecise data from the environment. This is why it is important to sieve what goes into us. King Solomon in all his wisdom teaches us in Proverbs 4:23, 'Above all, guard your heart, for everything you do flows from it.'

What you settle for will rule your life. Why settle for average when you can be phenomenal? Why live in a chicken coop when you can fly like an eagle? You are the gatekeeper of your destiny. You choose what stays in your life. Shut the door to ordinary and open your life to extraordinary. Choose inspiration, not expiration! -- Pastor Mensah Otabil

If you do not like what you are getting in life, change what you are putting into life. You are the master brewer!

CHAPTER 6

SELF RELIANCE

Each of us is a star. Sometimes we shine with the rest.
Sometimes we twinkle alone – Unknown

Self-reliance means to make one's own way; to do one's own work; to be independent; to take care of one's self; to better one's self by one's own effort and resources. Self-reliant people start from the bottom and work their way up. They improve their status without outside help.

Steven Harvey in his book, '*Act like a Lady, Think like a Man*', wrote the following:

'*Think about it: from the moment a boy is born, the first thing everyone around him starts doing is telling him what he must do to be a real man. He is taught to be tough—to wrestle, climb, get up without crying, not let anyone push him around.*

He is taught to work hard—to do chores around the house, get the groceries out of the car, take out the trash, shovel the snow, cut the grass, and as soon as he's old enough, get a job. He is taught to protect—to watch out for his mother and his younger siblings, to watch over the house and the family's property. And he is especially encouraged to uphold his family name—make something of himself so that when he walks in a room, everybody is clear about who he is, what he does, and how much he makes. Each of these things is taught in preparation for one thing: manhood.'

46

It is suggested in the above excerpt that right from cradle, the concept of self-reliance is inadvertently dissolved in the sub consciousness of mankind, and efforts made to prepare the individual to 'stand on his own'. Otherwise, man will crush under the ordeal of disappointment and despair.

Take for instance the life of lions in contrast to that of sheep. The life of a sheep is obviously easier than that of a lion. Sheep are given food and water freely by their shepherd, and are protected from predators by shelters they did not build. They fatten themselves on the shepherd's food, thriving into a multitude that outnumbers the lions.

These comforts, however, bind the sheep into slavery. They are bred to be weaker of mind and body; to require the shepherd's protection so greatly that they can be free of physical chains but never stray. Theirs is a lifetime of servitude — one that is comfortable but ends at the shepherd's whim. At sunset, the sheep are herded back into their prison and fed until they drift into sleep.

The lion enjoys no such promises, wandering upon the mountains in search of a meal; hungry, but free.

Some people choose to be like the sheep. They desire freedom but rely on others to provide their comforts, striving for riches but investing little effort to attain it. They scream in protest when they are fenced in and herded, angry that they are not free like the lions — but accept the shepherd's food nonetheless. Though they rebel by day, they always wander home to their cages by night.

Humans are not born as sheep or lions but must choose a path for themselves. Will you strive for what is easy and safe? To follow close to the multitude? To remain within the fences that protect you from the outside but imprison you within its boundaries? Or will you travel the path you choose, exploring freely in the dangerous forests of life, leading your own way in a planet filled with followers?

Though it lacks the comforts of a shepherd's security, a lion never wishes for the life of a sheep. A lion may hunger while a sheep is fed, but the fattest sheep is the lion's meal… no matter what.

Lions have no masters. They are their own masters. They are on their own. Though the lion must hunt for its own food and search for its own shelter, it is free to roam where it wishes and requires no one to open its gate. Although the feeding trough of the sheep is filled, it is only with the grass and grain of its master's choice. A lion must hunt and chase its meals, but feasts on anything it catches.

A lion has the choice of meal. The sheep does not. The lion is a master on his own. The sheep is a slave on his own. Which of these are you, a sheep or a lion? Is it the lion's stupidity that keeps it from a life of leisure? How can so many sheep be wrong as they grow fatter on the shepherd's food? Why would any creature choose to run free in the dangerous and uncertain wilderness?

They say good things come to those who wait but I say good things come to those who go out and make it happen – on their own!

Ralph Waldo Emerson, an American philosopher and essayist in 1841 wrote one of his famous essays entitled *Self Reliance*. A brief digest of that essay will go down well this this topic.

Throughout the write-up, he made a defence for the famous catch-phrase '*Trust thyself*' and insists that each person has his own self-contained genius, and that society and worldly influences must be resisted in favour of one's own individuality.

The concept of self-reliance, as taught by Emerson, needs to permeate our personalities because self-worth has great importance and value in our lives. A man who is self-reliant will be successful and any external influences would take away personal satisfaction.

He further indicates, **"It is said to be the age of the first person singular.**

> *Man is his own star; and the soul that can*
> *Render an honest and a perfect man,*
> *Commands all light, all influence, all fate;*
> *Nothing to him falls early or too late.*
> *Our acts our angels are, or good or ill,*
> *Our fatal shadows that walk by us still."*

Ralph Waldo Emerson (1841)

"Trust thyself: every heart vibrates to that iron string. Accept the place the divine providence has found for you, the society of your contemporaries, and the connection of events. Great men have always done so, and confided themselves childlike to the genius of their age, betraying

> *their perception that the absolutely trustworthy was seated at their heart, working through their hands, predominating in all their being.*"

What the writer sought to convey is that a man should follow what he thinks in order to discover his own ideals in life. You will be dispirited when you trail another man's path instead of your own. It can be likened to the bridle that goes into a horse's mouth, stacked on its head to direct it as desired by the rider. Horses under such conditions remain in perpetual restraint – they are not on their own!

One must pay attention to what is within his heart and act independently of others' opinions in order to bring satisfaction to one's self. No one can bring you peace, but yourself!

'The whole point of being alive is to evolve into the complete person you were intended to be' – Oprah Winfrey.

I have so much respect for entrepreneurs who do network marketing. They are a classical set of people who decide how much their worth is. They single headedly take their life into their own hands! How much they want to earn at what time is determined by them, and they work just towards that.

Wealth and success never come to those who simply wait for them to arrive. Look at how a single candle can defy darkness.

The value of self-expression also entreats us to follow individual will instead of conforming to social expectations. In today's world of global economic crunch, it behoves on us to desist from depending wholly on the government and political leaders to put food on our tables. Unemployment stares at thousands of graduates every now and then. They keep crushing under the heat of the system's failure due to over dependence.

Most believers of today also clasp their hands and await the fall of manna while they do little or no work. "God will provide," they say in anticipation for a miracle. Even in divine communication, God doesn't speak to us through prophets and priests anymore. By the bridge of this long-standing gap, Christ has given us direct access to the throne of God, that we may seek him always. To await the prophecies and prayers from the pulpit man is to be crippled fast. Talk to God – yourself!

Abraham Opoku-Baffour in his book, '*Called To Overcome*' suggests that '*Every overcomer must know what God wants him to do, and pursue it diligently. It is your responsibility to find out from God what he has prepared for you*'.

Why You Should Never Depend On Anyone But Yourself

A fact is that, you yourself are the only person that you can and ought to rely on. You may say that you have friends and a family that are willing to support you when you need help.

This may be true, but it does not change the fact that when push comes to shove you and the end is nigh, you are alone. As the saying goes, you come into this world alone and will depart from it alone.

You Are On Your Own

The sooner you come to accept this statement, the faster you will begin to rely on yourself for all that you need. A time is coming when friends will let you down, at least once in your

friendship. This is only human nature; we all make mistakes and poor decisions from time to time.

Even if your friends were always to have your back, you should keep in mind that they have their lives of their own. If you do not have complete, total guarantee of support from something, then you should not rely on it – by definition, it is not entirely reliable. If there's at least one situation in which your acquaintances will not be there for you, then you should conclude never to rely on people.

The reason why human beings are unreliable is that we are egocentric creatures. Our mental properties are focused on us, putting us ahead of others. This is not to say that you cannot put someone else ahead of yourself; but in order to do so you will have to be focused, with a strong intent.

We are built to survive on our own, yet cannot stay sane if isolated indefinitely – we both need and do not need other people. Nevertheless, one ought to learn how to rely on oneself.

CHAPTER 7

DESERTED, DEJECTED, DISAPPOINTED?

Pain and discomfort are always associated with the birth of a new thing. Keep pushing - Emmanuel Dei Tumi

T he model of self-authority, as dominating in this book, takes stimulus from the fact that, to be able to chart a course for your life, one has to develop active immunity to disillusionments and disappointments that come their way each day.

Facing frustrations leaves us hurt and sometimes broken but if we change our minds to view them as a source of growth, we will come to embrace them as a stepping stone to learning a lot about ourselves to achieve greater things in life.

The reality is that, as long as there is something for us to learn in life, we will continue to get hurt and be dejected. It therefore, becomes obligatory to shape our minds in pursuit of a successful life that is nevertheless conjugated with mistrust.

Think about it this way: in your struggle, only a few people care. The others are just curious. We always have the desire that everything will work for our good, but often that is not the case. In today's world of singularity and self-centredness, people cannot be trusted. Irrespective of your relationship with people, they would not spend their lives living for your good.

Even your own shadow will leave you eventually. In the beginning of the day is a tall, well figured shadow that pops out of your body. It becomes a companion that walks with you. It goes where you go, and promises to move with you through the thick and thin. It really does. But just when dusk approaches, you find yourself all alone. Your own shadow deserts you. In the end you are walking alone!

Creating a circle of hope and expectations around a spouse, a relative, friend, course mate or employer will be the panacea to being deserted, dejected and disappointed eventually. Never get too attached to anyone. It will lead to expectations – expectations will always lead to disappointment, and your world may come crushing. Expectation is the insidious worm that crawls around in our thoughts and destroys the dream or good intention we had in the first place. Of course, the afterthought is the original intention.

Anticipate everything and expect nothing – Unknown Author

Putting Temporary People in Permanent Places

Many of us believe it is better not to dream at all than to get our hopes up, only to fall. Well, if you live your life in fear of disappointment, you are not truly living. Disappointment has rather tricked you into playing it safe, and you will end with the very thing you sacrificed your life to avoid.

Disappointments are blessings in disguise if only we take time to think through and see how they serve as life teachers. If we aren't paying attention, our distress would rather begin to rule us – it would become our master if we do not have mastery over it.

The key to ducking this nuisance is just to slice off those that do not live up to expectation.

I quote the words of Prince Ea, a famous international musician and inspirer, *'Interacting with toxic people is like stepping in dog poop. Even after you try to clean it off your shoes, the smell will stay with you for a while, irritating you and the people close to you. Next time, just watch what you step and the company you keep.'*

Never put temporary people in the permanent places of your life. Do not be afraid of removing the wrong people from the right places of your life. It's your life. It's your right. Be bold to take such decisions concerning your life. If they call it pride, tell them it's your choice of class.

When things aren't adding up in your life; when people aren't completing the equation of your life, start subtracting.

Use this checker: Ask yourself, "Do these people support me, nurture me and encourage my creativity and ideas? Do they challenge me into becoming a better person?" If your answer is no, maybe it is time to replace such people.

Beware of dream killers – friends in most cases. It's sad to say this: these are the people who will be the first to try to talk you out of something that you are passionate about. Most of the people that have no dreams will wake up trying to talk you out of your dreams. They have no goals. They have nothing they are ambitious about.

We never lose friends. We only realise who the real ones are. If someone doesn't appreciate your presence, make them appreciate your absence. Life is too short to spend time thinking about someone who doesn't think about you. Stop putting an effort into those who show no effort towards you. Fake people kill your positivity.

Haven't you realised people change, and often become the people they said they will never be? Why not focus on where you are heading instead of putting your trust in a friend?

In the making of this book, starting from establishing an enterprise in whose name the project will be run till the release of this material, I have had to deal with countless cases of frustration from people who in one way or the other had a contribution to make. Graphic designers, artists, editors, promoters, entrepreneurs, journalists and friends whose services were needed at certain stages almost caused me my dreams. But for my burning desire to bring forth fruits from my conceived ideas, I have always been bent on achieving my goals. Anytime it was necessary to put sluggers aside, I did without hesitation and brought on people who would make my dreams come true. More often than not, I did things by myself.

The outcome of the career you envision is based on your response to disappointment. For every level, there's another devil, therefore if the things around you aren't changing, change the things around you.

Stand on your own like a star and make your own light. It's better to not expect much. It will give you great results if you do not focus on the material details and live in your fantasy even when others tell you your life isn't right.

Humans can be very wily, self-centred and egotistical. For me, it's the dream and its challenges that give me the thrill of my life.

No one wants to be disappointed by others. But we will, if we perpetually raise expectations that people will live their lives for the benefit of ours. Some people will give you good advice; listen to them. Others do not know what they're talking about; learn to distinguish between the two. You will know in your gut when others' advice is sound.

Two things you need to kill in your life – TRUST and EXPECTATION. This would be that great step that leads you to becoming what you want to. Trust is the hardest thing to find and the easiest thing to lose.

Expect less. You will end up really disappointed if you think people will do for you as you do for them. Expectations cloud your focus and places before you an illusion of hope; a false perception of aid. Not everyone has the same heart as yours. No expectations. No disappointment.

Do not be quick to trust claims people make. Most of the time, they have no idea what they are confidently saying. Having doubts is key to not losing trust.

Laugh with many, don't trust any.

When men desert us, all we need is a word of encouragement, instead of retiring. We should embrace each storm and learn from them. The mud, the whirlwind, the storm, the haze, the rain and the uncomfortable moments people take us through are meant to be faced.

Making the Most Out Of the Woes

Whatever it is you are going though, I want you to know that you are exactly where you need to be. Take a look at the lotus plant. They say it is the most beautiful, fragrant flower on the face of the earth. But the funny thing is, it was borne out of the nasty, dirty, ugly swamp; the swamp; the mud!

You do not grow lotus on the marbles or in the highlands – only from the swamp can these flowers emerge. Accept the fact that you are the lotus. All the ugly situations; your past, the struggle, the strife; are necessary. You need these situations to become what you are destined to be. That is greatness. Hold your ground. Keep moving forward out of the mud and you will sail through. The strongest trees grow in the strongest winds, not the best soil!

The experience you gain is your lesson. The life you make out of it is your blessing. Always remember that the teacher teaches a lesson that becomes a blessing.

Your better days lie ahead of you. Just hold on – Kemi Sogunle

You want to give up? You want to sob yourself in dismay? Find out how many dogs the Russians sent to space before man walked in space. Ask about how many times inventors had to go over in disappointment; how many times Thomas Edison had to kill his disappointment to come up with the electric light bulb.

'Our greatest weakness lies in giving up. The most certain way to succeed is always to try one more time' – Thomas Edison

Progress is like autopsy – you find out where you went wrong and then give it another try. Progress is doing it again because you failed to make something out of nothing.

You can have feelings about your failure because it is sad but you can't make it tear you apart. You need to rise up and work again to succeed. Being successful doesn't mean everything is perfect. It means that you have decided to look beyond the imperfections. Hope for the best and stick with it day in day out. Even when you get tired, even when you want to walk away, don't! You are a pioneer. And nobody ever said it will be easy.

Our growth in life happens when circumstances are the most uncertain. The uncertain times cause us to rely more on God.

In the movie *Top Gun*, Tom Cruise plays Maverick, a young, talented and cocky aviator who dreams of being the premier pilot in the U.S Navy. In the opening scenes of the film, Maverick showcases his flying ability but also displays a knack for pushing the envelope with regards to safety.

Midway through the movie, Maverick's characteristic aggression spells disaster. His plane crashes, killing his best friend and co-pilot. Although cleared of wrongdoing, the painful memory of the accident haunts him. He quits taking risks and loses his edge. Struggling to regain his poise, he considers giving up on his dream. The incident nearly wrecks Maverick's career, but he eventually reaches within to find the strength to return to the sky.

Like Maverick, many of us live with the memory of failure embedded in our psyche. Perhaps a business we started went bankrupt, or we were fired from a position. Disappointment is the gap that exists between expectation and reality, and all of us have encountered that gap.

Even the snails, shell-pads and chameleons, despite how slow they are… reach their destinations.

CHAPTER 8

THE UNLIMITED POWER IN YOU

Behind me is an infinite power. Before me is in an endless possibility, around me is a boundless opportunity - Unknown

The gold fish is a special type of aquatic life whose growth can only be limited by the size of the container in which it finds itself and the quality of the water. In other words, the bigger the size of the tank within which it lives, the bigger it grows. The smaller the size of the tank, the smaller it grows.

In 2008, Widow Ada Shaw, a British marine biologist, reported about a gold fish he bought when it was just an inch long having grown to become 1ft 3in long. If the second largest gold fish in the world had been placed in a smaller tank, it would not have grown to that size.

The conditions influencing the growth of the gold fish is akin to the conditions that surround the personal growth and achievement of a human being. The gold fish has no limits in itself with respect to its evolution. In terms of your potential to grow, achieve and succeed in life, there is no limit on you.

The Chinese bamboo tree is unique in its germination and growth. It takes four years to germinate after planting the seed but once it sprouts, it grows to 80 feet in six years. Another uniqueness I have discovered about bamboo tree is that, it grows as big as it can, depending on the space available to it. In other words, the bigger you want it to be, the greater the space you should make available. For instance, to reach its full height, the bamboo tree must have an area of at least 30 feet in circumference available!

The only limit is the one you permit your environment or the space in which you live and operate to place on you. You can grow to become as big as you desire. You can excel as far as you desire and work for. If you permit limitations, they will always limit you.

Taking Up the Task to Self-Actualisation

Having your divine purpose in mind, your mission is the mission you give yourself. No directions, no prescriptions, no limitations – its free range, and you are on your own! There are absolutely no limits to this. We are unrestricted beings with no ceiling on our roofs. The capabilities and power that is within every individual are boundless.

We have to pilot our own dreams; we cannot entrust them to anyone else. People who aren't following their own dreams resent to pursuing ours. Such people feel inadequate when others succeed so they try to drag them down. If we listen to external forces, we allow our dreams to be hijacked. At a point, other people will place limitations on us, doubting our own abilities.

There are going to be countless times in your life when you will feel down and you will feel like giving up. The voice in your head will tell you to stop and you will start to doubt yourself, but never listen to that voice. Be strong and keep moving on. Never give up on yourself. You have to keep on going and eventually you will reach your destination. And when you do, you will realize how much more powerful you have become.

"We all have different things that we go through in our everyday life, and it's really important to know just at the end of the day, it doesn't matter what you face, you know that you're going to win at the end of the day. You've got to believe in yourself. You've got to believe in God, know that He's going to get you through it." – Kelly Rowland.

Recognise the things that trap your dreams and overcome them. A lot of us never see our dreams come true. Instead of soaring through the clouds, our dreams languish like broken-down airplane confined to its hangar.

When surrounded by the turbulence of criticism, we have to grasp the control tightly to keep us from being knocked off course. We are indeed endowed with the power to do so.

Bob Proptor, a philosopher said, *'If you do just a little research it will be evident to you that anyone that accomplished anything did not know how they were going to do it. They only knew they were going to do it.'*

There's this story that was told about an audience at a seminar. The speaker, after a lengthy talk took out a fifty cedis note and asked the audience, "Who wants this money?" Everyone sat, screaming "Me, Me, Me!" In the middle of the chants sprang a lady who ran up to him and snatched the money. The others merely sat raising their hands whiles the lady took the bold step to grab the enviable bounty.

This is the time to pick up the mantle. Let your action be louder than your voice. We are too relaxed waiting for prospects that are already staring at us right in the face. The universe likes speed! Do not delay. Do not second-guess. Do not doubt when the opportunity is there and the impulse is kicking. When you have inspired thought, you have to trust it, and then move. When the intuitive nudge pushes you, act! It is your life!

Always, the key to making progress is to recognise how to take that very first step with all the supremacy vested in you. One day you will need to be that person who changed the face of the corner where you are. When you look beyond the narrow horizon you will get to an unexpected end.

Your spirit is so big. It fills a room. You are like Aladdin's Genie! You are energy. You have the power to do what it takes to break through any obstacles that stand in the way of yourself, your dreams, and your happiness. Keep in mind your command is unconstrained.

CHAPTER 9

YOU ARE YOUR OWN PROBLEM – LOOK WITHIN YOURSELF

People that have issues only need to look in the mirror –
Shannon L. Alder

I want you to meet the person responsible for your woes; the debauched spirit who has been haunting you; the chauffeur of the vehicle carrying your endless terrors. I have a tip-off of who's to blame for all your miseries. There's that somebody orchestrating your misfortunes.

You need not look far. Get a mirror. Hold it up high to your head level and look into it. Shannon L. Alder said, "People that have issues only need to look in the mirror. There they will meet the one person that will betray them the most."

YOU!

You are your problem because you make your own choices. You use your own words, and have the autonomy to make decisions. The responsibility is yours, and it starts with developing a belief or habit that you, as an individual, are accountable for any outcome; even where others are involved. This goes further to iterate that you own an obligation to take action and deliver results for your own welfare.

How easy and convenient is it for us to blame everything and everybody for the things that have gone on in our lives! Most

66

people wake up every day looking for pain, dysfunction, utility tariff hikes and unemployment to blame for their unsuccessfulness. They look for a way to blame their excuses on their unfortunate childhood happenings. They hold the belief that their families are somewhat responsible for their stagnations.

We are being raised as a generation of people who can cook up excuses as to why they are not winning. We apportion blames every now and then without looking within ourselves to assess our inputs.

Cigarette and tobacco packages come with graphic warnings that are made visible enough to increase the consumer's knowledge about the drastic health consequences of using such toxins. For each image there's an accompanying health message in explanation. The manufacturer confesses to you that smoking will kill you. You have heard of cancer, lung diseases, heart diseases, stroke and brain damage – the list is endless. But for you, it's a 'Never mind!' You will smoke and puff with pride. You will ignore the caution and consume the thousands of poisons without panic.

In 2014, the World Health Organisation enlisted in this order: Ischemic Heart Disease, Stroke, Lower Respiratory Infections, HIV/AIDS, and Lung Cancer as the most common causes of death globally. A hundred percent of these killer diseases are dominating because of our own actions. We die from our own lifestyle. The Biopsychosocial Model says, the individual must be involved in the treatment of his diseases because he is part of the cause, literally.

People will use all manner of drugs and substances, go through all sorts of procedures, and treat their bodies in all manner of ways, just to earn pleasure. We should point accusing fingers at ourselves and bow in shame!

Before you blame an illness, deformity or death on a dwarf, a wizard or a poor old woman, look within yourself. Find your oppressor in a mirror!

Some people are like rudderless boats on the ocean completely at the mercy of the tides to take them where they are going. They end up where they do not want to be. Sooner or later, the shifting currents will run them to the ground, breaking them on rocks!

You cannot subtract 5 from 3 and have 2. You know why? That is atypical. It is an attempt to beat the principles of nature. When you compel yourself to squeeze 5 units out of 3, it will repel until it appears you are succeeding. You may end up with a figure of 3. But it will be negative. Negative 3! Then negativity will be staring at you. You will now have to contend with the results that are undesirable – results that are on the left side of life.

By recognising the difference between fault and responsibility, we can eschew the blame game and take ownership of difficult problems. Live with responsibility and make yourself stronger and more action-oriented.

Regard your life as something over which you have control, rather than something that just happens to you. To overcome problems and achieve lasting happiness, we must look inward and understand how we continually thwart our own well-being by giving in to feelings and thoughts that cause us pain.

Stop being a lazy being; full of excuses. You are the reason you are not winning. You keep messing with negative, evil and dysfunctional people and expect positive results. Stop looking at your potbelly when you get out of bed. Stop complaining about the way you look when you are eating everything and never going to the gym.

You are the reason you look the way you look. You are the reason you are unemployed. You are the reason why your surroundings are so unproductive. You refuse to get yourself on the go because you kill your own dreams; because you are crushing yourself with trivialities.

Life is made up of seeds and harvests. We reap what we sow. What you are today is a reflection of what you have sown yesterday. If you sow promiscuity, you will reap death, diseases and basket full of fatherless babies. If you sow confusion, you will reap chaos. If you sow impulse-buying, you will reap debts. If you sow in crime, you will reap in crime.

It is true that sometimes we can't be responsible for what we have no control over, but it is also worth noting that control comes from our choices and responses.

You may not be responsible for your conception but you are certainly accountable for your development. You may not be responsible for your birth but you are accountable for your growth. You may not be responsible for choosing your family, but you are certainly accountable for choosing your future spouse. You may not be responsible for your struggles, but you are certainly accountable for your breakthrough.

We become the source of our problems when we fail to mount a befitting response to the negativities over whose occurrence we may not have control. You are your own problem if you remain in the struggles.

Even though we are in an era of high technological advancements with the advent of support systems, premature deaths have become as common as pillows on beds.

Our overall quality of life has not become any better. Life gets worse by day. Because we have not realised the extent to which our actions and inactions impact on our lives, we do not look within ourselves for solutions.

During one of my clinical attachments at a hospital, I had the opportunity of being on a case of a middle-aged woman with diabetes. She needed to get her right leg amputated in order to save her life. When the attending doctor mentioned the extent of her damage and the indication for the said surgery, she broke into tears and fell to the ground, lamenting. Her demeanour posited that a certain family member had caused this harm spiritually. According to her, she maintains a high suspicion that, that person had a hand in her ill-health.

But apparently, this patient was a non-attendant who had defaulted treatment for more than two years, and now had to suffer the complications of poor compliance.

Some people get emotional satisfaction from talking about how terrible other people are. But research has found that when you talk negatively about how awful a colleague is, the listening friend is more likely to associate the negativity to you rather than to the person you are describing. This is called 'spontaneous trait transference'. So it is best to go easy on bad-mouthing others because it many backfire, anyway.

It takes a wise person to accept outwardly and inwardly that they screwed up. I am not saying we should never blame others. Sometimes others are at fault and they need to know it and take responsibility. But being able to accept blame when necessary means we actually become less helpless and passive.

If everything is someone else's fault, then what part do I play in my own life? Are my actions entirely without consequence? Am I that powerless? Or do all my actions only lead to good outcomes?

Knowing we accept responsibility when things go wrong means we can also accept credit when things go well. We do, as individuals have an effect on life, and that is a good thing.

But we need to develop capacity to be objective enough about ourselves to avoid assuming we could never possibly have created problems ourselves. We also need to distinguish between accepting responsibility and punishing ourselves unduly.

There is absolutely no shame in being able to admit to yourself or others that you made mistakes. Quite opposite, it shows real strength of character.

CHAPTER 10

THE WAY REMAINS FORWARD

Stop being who you were and become who you are – Paulo Coelho

God did not create failure when He formed you. He did not breathe His life into a mistake. Remove anything that creates a picture of failure in your thoughts and choose to see yourself succeeding. In your day-to-day activities, cultivate positive beliefs about yourself and your excitement and happiness will become contagious. What you should do all the time is follow your passion and enthusiasm.

Success is reserved only for those who believe they can succeed.

Preserve the impression that you are born to add value to this word to heal and make it a better place. See the good in yourself and focus on it only. Before you lies a resounding victory which you needn't take your gaze off. It yearns for your concentration.

What you value determines what you focus on. If your number one value of life is security, I guarantee that you are likely to check around a building for weak spot, the moment you enter. It literally controls what you notice or do not notice. It's not an obsessive compulsive disorder. It's focus! That means you need to centre your mind on the things that matter to you most.

Change Precedes The Way Forward

Having been exposed to a myriad range of intuition,

72

reformation is now a key requisite to propelling you into a resolute being. Never be afraid to start all over again. This is a brand new opportunity to rebuild what you truly want.

It also means giving up on the old personality that was stuffed with complaints, criticisms, displeasure, inferiority complex and stress. Giving up doesn't mean you are weak. It means you are smart enough to let go and move on. Let go of your old self.

There is the need to make a conscious effort towards a new life. Change is a necessity. Without it, we never grow. Without it, butterflies would remain in a wriggling state of a cocoon forever.

It is the only final step to self-actualisation following a decision to be what you want to become. Do not fear change. You may lose something good, but you may also gain something great.

The past cannot be changed, forgotten, edited or erased. It can only be accepted. If through a broken heart, God can bring His purposes to pass in the world, then thank the people who broke your heart.

You can't change the seasons. You can't alter the trends, you can't change the economy. The long-standing traditions of society are too entrenched to adjust. But you can change from that overly dependent being to a more self-owning person.

Today is the day you need to part ways with the circumstances that keep you lagging behind, the people that make you feel inadequate and the situations that make you a slug. The failures have come and gone. You must get back up again. Those are the dark moments that are yet to make way for the brighter days. Without the dark we will never see the stars.

I can't go back to yesterday, because I was a different person then – Lewis Carrol

A Creed To Live By

You have the power to do what it takes to break through any obstacles that stand in the way of yourself, your dreams, and your happiness. Take full charge of your life and people will look at you and say, 'What do you do differently from me'?

I see a future of unbounded potentials in unrestrained possibilities. The power accompanying your existence is emerging within you, it will take over your life, and it will feed you. Eventually, all things fall into place. Until then laugh at the confusion, live for the moments, and know everything happens for a reason. Accept that the challenges are for you to face – alone!

Ps. Oscar-Faithway of Apostolic Mission said, "*Anything that irritates you is walking you through a journey of patience. Anyone who abandons you is teaching you how to stand up to your own feet. Anything that causes you rage is teaching you*

> *about forgiveness and compassion. Anything that has power over you is teaching you how to take your power back. Anything you hate is teaching you unconditional love. Anything you fear is teaching you courage to overcome your fear. Anything you can't control is teaching you how to let go. Life is learning....Learn the right way!"*

As for your visions, keep them up high. Just a day if you do not give up on your dreams, you also will reach your goals. Never give up for as the adage goes, quitters never win and winners never quit.

Someday, you will need to be celebrated for your unsung heroism, so be inspired to work out your redemption. You must do the things which you think you cannot do. You will be successful one day, keep on trying till all walls are broken and crushed down. Just don't forget, failure and winning are all state of minds.

You should be that person that life happens to. It doesn't matter what the current state of the economy is. You have the confidence to beat your chest and say, "This is the passion that's burning inside of me. This is the transition of the revolution I want to create".

The wise man is the one who takes courageously the step right ahead of him, planting his foot firmly and confidently upon it. Although he is unable to see further ahead. The waiting business is a poor policy. Don't wait for something to turn up. Go out and turn something up.

Every day when you wake up, you have two options: you can look at your alarm clock and hit the snooze and go back to bed. And do what? And dream about what you want to do with your comfortable pillow. Or you can look at the clock and kick it, and get up, and go pursue your dreams.

I dare you to get up, I dare you to chase your dreams. I dare you to give yourself value, I dare you to spend time to explore who you are so you can find out what you do that nobody does. I dare you to become an asset. I double-dare you to invest in yourself – in your mind!

When you become the right person, what you do is, you show your value.

You were created with a specific purpose, a specific design. You are special. When you become the right person, you being to separate yourself from other people. You become unique.

Everything will be alright. Maybe not today, but eventually. You have a dream inside of you, a dream you have hidden from the world. You've made excuses for it and delayed it. There are a million things never realised and several achievements yet to be made. To establish true self-esteem we must concentrate on our successes and forget about the failures and the negativities in our lives. It's your life. Don't let anyone make you feel guilty for living it your way.

When your memory is full of sadness and your life is covered with scars of abuse and pain, don't look back, but look ahead. When tears start rolling in your face and your struggles seem to be overwhelming you, don't look back, but look ahead. When people walk away from you and some even betray your trust, don't look back, but look ahead. When your faith is shaking and your hope seem to be dying like a candle light, don't look back but look ahead.

Visualise your desired future and don't even look back to picture your past. The way remains forward!

Muse on what this book exposes to you and you can imagine what you can do from this day forward. How will you seize the moments? How will you dance to your music? How will you write the story of your life? Well, nobody has answers to these questions. Just find them. It's your life and you are on your own!

In conclusion, every man must be able to accomplish their assigned task in an independent resourceful, self-sufficient manner without making a fuss. **Every tub must stand on its own bottom**. Everyone must take care of himself, everyone must paddle his own canoe.

Life is phenomenal, it's a magnificent trip. Enjoy it!

> *The darkest part of the night is just before dawn*
> *Be bold always, it pays.*
> *Dreams give support to hope.*
> *Hope inspires efforts.*
> *Effort results in success.*
> *So dreams are the root of success.*
> *May all your dreams come true.*

You have spent the past times in a womb. You have shared nutrients with a 'mother'. She has literally lived your life for you. She ate for you. She gave you all the protection. Your life was largely full of inactivity, sleep, and dependence.

Birth time is now! The time to be pushed you into a new world is due. Take a peep, and see people impatiently waiting to welcome you. You mean so much to them. Make a loud cry to announce your presence when you get there.

If you are ready, shall we clump and cut off the umbilical cord? I guess you know what that means…

THE END

"If you can't fly then run, if you can't run then walk, if you can't walk then crawl, but whatever you do, you have to keep moving forward."

– Martin Luther King Jr.

AXIOMS

- To conquer fear is the beginning of wisdom – Bertrand Russell
- Let your imagination run wild with the possibilities of everything you could explore and experience immediately – Tony Robbins
- Do you want to know who you are? Don't ask. Act! Action will delineate and define you – Thomas Jefferson
- If there's no struggle, there is no progress – Frederick Douglass
- Vision is the art of seeing the invisible – Jonathan Swift
- Things turn out best for people who make the best of the way things turn out.
- Surround yourself only with people who are on the same mission as you
- The only person you should strive to be better than, is the person you were yesterday.
- They always say times changes things, but you actually have to change them yourself.
- One resolution I have made and try always to keep is to rise above the little things – John Burroughs
- Losing is a learning experience. It teaches you humility. It is also a powerful motivator

- If you set out to be less than you are capable, you will be unhappy for the rest of your life – Abraham Marslow
- You are never too old to chase your dreams – Diana Nyad
- Don't be afraid to be unique or speak your mind, because that's what makes you different from everyone else – Dave Thomas
- I failed on my way to success – Thomas Edison
- No one succeeds without effort. Those who succeed owe their success to perseverance – Ramana Maharshi
- Do your little bits of good where you are; it's those little things put together that overwhelm the world – Desmond Tutu
- Remember you are unique. If that is not fulfilled, then something wonderful has been lost – Martha Graham
- Once we accept our limits, we go beyond them – Brendan Francis
- A man, as a general rule owes very little to what he's born with. A man is what he makes of himself.
- We cannot become what we need to be, by remaining what we are – Max Dupree

- There's the popular saying that life is 10% what happens to you and 90% how you handle it

- Success is like building blocks – you make one, then another follows. Just take that first step!

- If you want to stand out, don't just be different. Be outstanding.

- To get what you want, stop doing what isn't working – Dennis Weaver

- Good ideas are not adopted automatically. They must be driven into practice with courageous patience – Hyman Rickover

- They always say time changes things. But you actually have to change them yourself – Andy Warhol

- A little more persistence, a little more effort, and what seemed hopeless failure may turn to glorious success.

- It's hard to fail, but it's worse never to have tried to succeed

- Nothing is built on stone – all is built on sand. But we must build as if the sand were stone – Humphrey Bogart

- I will love the light for it shows me the way, yet I will endure the darkness because it shows me the stars.

- I have the simplest tastes. I am always satisfied with the best – Oscar Wilde

- Whatever the mind can conceive and believe, the mind can – Napoleon Hill
- To escape fear, you have to go through it, not around it – Richie Norton
- All that we are is the result of what we have thought. It is founded on our thoughts and made up of our thoughts – Buddha
- You are valuable and irreplaceable. If you are told otherwise, do not believe it.
- Do what you can, with what you have, where you are – Theodore Roosevelt
- Be the type of person you want to meet
- Your talent is God's gift to you. What you do with it is your gift back to God.
- I am in charge of how I feel and today, I am choosing HAPPINESS
- Never be afraid of taking unfamiliar paths because sometimes they are the ones that takes us to the best places – Emmanuel Dei Tumi
- Never bend your head. Always hold it high. Look the world straight in the eye' – Hellen Keller
- To conquer fear is the beginning of wisdom – Bertrand Russell
- You can't let other people tell you who you are. You have to decide that for yourself

- Without the dark we will never see the stars
- Always do what you are afraid to do. – Ralph Waldo Emerson
- Only a few people care. The others are just curious.
- Don't be afraid to start over. It is a brand opportunity to rebuild what you truly want.
- The past cannot be changed, forgotten, edited or erased. It can only be accepted
- The greatest thing to fear is your own fears
- Each of us is a star. Sometimes we shine with the rest. Sometimes we twinkle alone.
- When things aren't adding up in your life, when people aren't completing the equation of your life, start subtracting. Be on your own!
- Train your mind to see the good in yourself.
- Don't ask God to guide your footsteps if you're not ready to take the step into success
- Stop looking for reasons to be unhappy. Focus on your things you do have, and the reasons you should be happy.
- I was always looking outside myself for strength and confidence but it comes from within. It was here all the time – Anna Fred
- I don't know the key for success but the key to failure to trying to please everybody. Bill Cosby

- Prove yourself to yourself, not others.
- But do not let he shadows of the past darken the doorstep of your future.
- Why compare yourself to others? No one in the entire world can do a better job of being you than you.
- Look at how a single candle can both defy and define the darkness
- If you desire to make a difference in the world, you must be different from the world.
- You never know how strong you are until being strong is the only choice you have.
- I'm not afraid of storms, for I'm learning how to sail my ship. – Louisa May Alcott
- Don't let the fear of striking out hold you back. – Babe Ruth
- Nothing in life is to be feared. It is only to be understood. – Marie Curie
- The brave man is not he who does not feel afraid, but he who conquers that fear. – Nelson Mandela
- Decide that you want it more than you are afraid of it. – Bill Cosby

BIBLIOGRAPHY / REFERENCES

Law of Attraction, www.thesecret.tv
The Master Brewer, Lade Wosornu
Self-Reliance, Ralph Waldo Emerson, 1841
Essential Tips To Face Your Fears, Tinybuddha.com, Tess Marshall
Apocalypto Movie Review, Iron And Iron
Called To Overcome, Abraham O. Baffour
How To Be Yourself, Your True Self, Advanced Life Skills
Hook, Line and Sinner; Grey's Anatomy S06E20

NOTES

www.ingramcontent.com/pod-product-compliance
Lightning Source LLC
Chambersburg PA
CBHW032147040426
42449CB00005B/427